W9-BAX-277

NATURE DETECTIVE

Plants

ANITA GANERI

Illustrated by Adrian Lascom

FRANKLIN WATTS
NEW YORK · LONDON · TORONTO · SYDNEY

© 1992 Franklin Watts

First published in the United States
in 1992 by
Franklin Watts, Inc.
95 Madison Avenue
New York, NY10016

Library of Congress Cataloging-in-Publication Data

Ganeri, Anita, 1961–
    Plants / by Anita Ganeri.
      p.   cm. — (Nature detective)
    Includes index.
    Summary: Illustrations with explanatory text provide information
about various types of plants and how and where they grow. Includes
simple projects.
    ISBN 0-531-14194-2
    1. Plants—Miscellanea—Juvenile literature. 2. Plants—
Identification—Juvenile literature. [1. Plants. 2. Plants—
—Identification.] I. Title. II. Series: Nature detective (New
York, N.Y.)
QK49.G35 1992   91–39806
581—dc20   CIP AC

Designer: Splash Studio
Editor: Sarah Ridley
Additional illustrations: Danny Flynn (cover and title page)
and Terry Pastor

Printed in Belgium.

The publishers regret that they
have been unable to show the plants
in this book drawn to scale.

Contents

What is a plant?

Plants came before all animal life on earth. The first plantlike organisms lived in the sea over 3,000 million years ago. They were blue green algae, plants which are still found in water today. Without them, there could have been no animal life on Earth. This is because plants, in making food for themselves, give off oxygen which animals need to breathe.

The first land plants appeared about 400 million years ago. They had no flowers, leaves, or roots. The first flowering plants appeared some 300 million years later.

Today, there are over 375,000 species of plant. They range from tiny, single-celled algae to huge sequoia trees, over 270 feet tall. About 250,000 of these species are flowering plants, like the buttercup shown on the right.

Plants also give us some of our food, medicine, clothes, and other everyday things. You will see plants, or plant products, all around you. Start your detective work by looking around your house, yard, or park.

The types of plants

Plants are divided up into several different groups, depending on whether they have flowers, how they reproduce, and so on. The plants shown here are not to scale.

Fungi There are about 50,000 species of fungi. They include mushrooms, toadstools, and molds.

Conifers These nonflowering plants produce their seeds in cones. Pine trees and Norway spruce fall into this group.

Mosses and liverworts Both of these simple land plants reproduce by spores. They have no flowers or roots. This plant is a liverwort.

Flowering plants These are plants that produce true flowers, for example broad-leaved trees, poppies, and grasses. Flowering plants form by far the biggest single group of plants.

Lichens A combination of algae and fungi make up lichens, such as the rust-colored or gray crusts you can sometimes see on trees, rocks, and walls.

Ferns and horsetails These nonflowering plants do not make seeds, but reproduce with spores. Ferns have large fronds growing from their underground stems.

Algae Algae are very simple nonflowering plants, mostly found in water. They range from one-celled organisms to huge seaweeds.

A buttercup

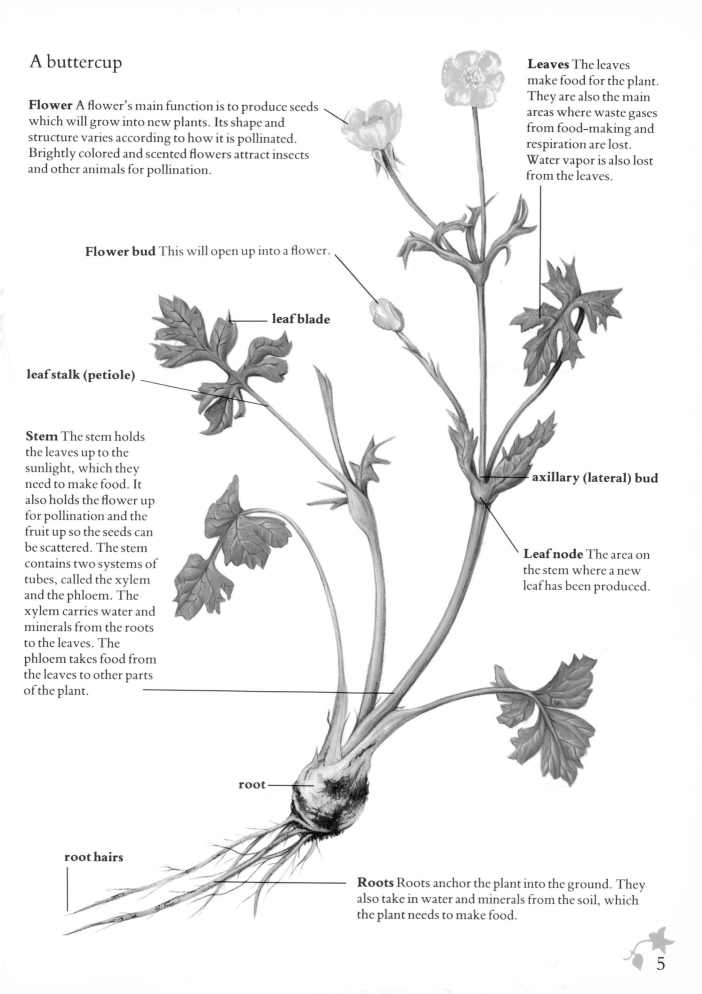

Flower A flower's main function is to produce seeds which will grow into new plants. Its shape and structure varies according to how it is pollinated. Brightly colored and scented flowers attract insects and other animals for pollination.

Leaves The leaves make food for the plant. They are also the main areas where waste gases from food-making and respiration are lost. Water vapor is also lost from the leaves.

Flower bud This will open up into a flower.

leaf blade

leaf stalk (petiole)

Stem The stem holds the leaves up to the sunlight, which they need to make food. It also holds the flower up for pollination and the fruit up so the seeds can be scattered. The stem contains two systems of tubes, called the xylem and the phloem. The xylem carries water and minerals from the roots to the leaves. The phloem takes food from the leaves to other parts of the plant.

axillary (lateral) bud

Leaf node The area on the stem where a new leaf has been produced.

root

root hairs

Roots Roots anchor the plant into the ground. They also take in water and minerals from the soil, which the plant needs to make food.

Where do plants live?

Plants live almost everywhere in the world, from windswept mountain slopes to the hottest deserts. You will see them in towns and cities, on a walk through the countryside or along the beach, in your own backyard and on wasteland. There are very few places where you will not be able to look at them closely.

Plants are able to live in such a wide range of habitats because they can make their own food (see pages 10-11). Many of them also have special features to help them survive, such as waxy leaf coatings to stop them drying out, defensive spines and hairy leaves and stems for insulation.

Deciduous woodland

These are some of the plants which you might see in a deciduous wood. Deciduous trees shed their leaves in winter to survive the harsh weather.

1 Beech Beech trees can grow up to 100 feet high. They have smooth, silvery bark and oval, pointed leaves. In autumn, their leaves turn a rich orange red color and drop to the ground.

2 Sulfur tuft This very common fungus grows in clusters, or tufts, at the base of deciduous trees. The best time to look for it is in the autumn.

3 Wood anemone Many woodland plants, including the wood anemone, flower early in spring before the trees come into leaf and shade out the sunlight which they need to make food.

4 Common blue violet

Coniferous woodland

Conifers produce cones, and are usually evergreen which means that they do not shed their leaves in autumn. They are well suited to colder places. Heavy snow slides off their sloping branches instead of breaking them. Few plants can grow under conifers due to the lack of sunlight reaching through the trees and the lack of nutrients in the ground.

1 Douglas fir This tall, fast-growing conifer is often farmed for its timber. It has the typical pyramid shape of many types of conifers. Its pine needle leaves are springy and scented.

2 Saffron milk-cap This common fungus is seen in late summer and autumn under conifers, particularly pine trees. If its flesh is broken, a bright orange "milk" oozes out. The milk turns deep red after about 30 minutes.

3 Wood sorrel This woodland plant has leaves which look like clover leaves. To survive the cold, these fold up in bad weather and at night.

4 Scotch pine

5 Bracken

Moorland and bog plants

Many types of plants have adapted to the combination of wet and windy conditions and acid soil of moorlands and bogs. Look out for these plants growing in boggy areas.

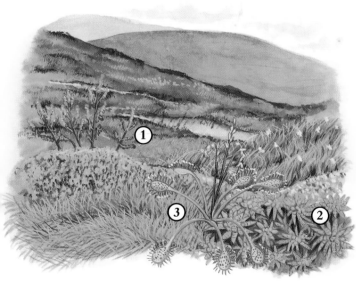

1 Heather Heather thrives in acidic moorland soil where it grows in low clumps, out of the wind. It will grow on the drier areas of boggy land.
2 Sphagnum moss This moss grows in bogs. It soaks up water, giving it a spongy feel. As it rots, it gradually turns into peat.
3 Sundew Sundews live in damp, boggy places. They make their own food but also trap insects to eat. The insects land on their sticky leaves which fold around them. The plant then digests their bodies.

Seashore plants

Many different plants can be found on the seashore. Some live on the sea cliffs, or in shallow water, others on the pebbly or sandy beaches. Many seashore plants have tough leaves to protect themselves from the salt spray.
Look out for these plants living on sand dunes.

1 Marram grass This spiky grass is usually the first plant to start growing on sand dunes. Its roots bind the sand together and help to stop the sand dunes from blowing away. Once this grass is established, other plants can grow on the dunes as well.

2 Yellow horned poppy The bright flowers of this plant only last two days. It lives on sand dunes and shingle shores and has a very long seed pod.

3 Couch grass   4 Sea bindweed

Pond, river and lake plants

Freshwater habitats provide a variety of homes for plants. Oxygen produced by the leaves of floating and submerged plants dissolves in the water and is used by water creatures. The marshy area around some ponds and lakes also creates ideal conditions for certain plants.

1 Water crowfoot The crowfoot's underwater leaves are long and feathery so that they can take up as much sunlight and carbon dioxide as possible, and yet do not get torn by water currents.
2 Weeping willow The weeping willow has curved branches which hang over the water. The leaves fall in the water and rot, providing important nutrients.
3 Duckweed Duckweed forms a floating carpet of tiny leaves over the surface of ponds. Each leaf has a tiny root trailing in the water below.
4 Yellow iris   5 Cattail

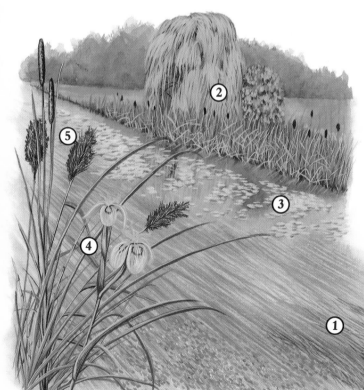

Garden plants

A good place to start studying plants is in your own backyard or local park. Many of these plants grow in the wild, too.

1 Bindweed Bindweed is a wildflower that climbs along fences and railings, and is very difficult to remove. It has white, cornet-shaped flowers which are pollinated by moths.

2 Daisy Daisies can be found almost all the year round. They grow on lawns, in meadows and by the roadside. There are several different varieties.

3 Lavender Lavender bushes are very popular in gardens because of their fragrance. In warm countries, especially around the Mediterranean, lavender thrives on dry, stony hillsides.

4 Crab apple tree   5 Rose

Plant spotting

You don't need very much equipment to study plants, but some of the items below might be useful. There are a few rules to remember, though. Never pick or uproot wildflowers. Many are becoming very rare as their habitats are being destroyed.

Field guide Take this with you, so that you can identify plants without picking them.

Notebook, pencil, and ruler A quick sketch of a plant makes a useful record and can be used for identification later on. Make a note of the plant's size, the color and shape of its flowers and leaves, where and when you saw it, and details of other plants growing nearby.

Magnifying lens A folding pocket lens is excellent for looking at details of plants. It should have a magnification of × 7.

Camera If you have a camera, taking photographs is a good way of keeping an accurate record of the plants you see. Don't forget to keep a note of the photos you have taken, with details of the time of day and year, location, and weather.

How do plants grow?

Animals have to search out food to eat, but since plants cannot move around, most make their own food. They can do this because their leaves contain a special green pigment called chlorophyll. The chlorophyll uses energy absorbed from sunlight to turn carbon dioxide and water into a simple sugar for the plant to live on. This process is called photosynthesis. Its waste product is oxygen which we all need to breathe.

Leaves also contain red, yellow, and orange pigments, usually hidden by the chlorophyll. In the autumn, chlorophyll in deciduous trees breaks down and the leaves change color, before they die and fall off.

How photosynthesis works

oxygen out

sunlight

carbon dioxide in

water in

minerals in

simple sugar made in leaves

Inside a leaf

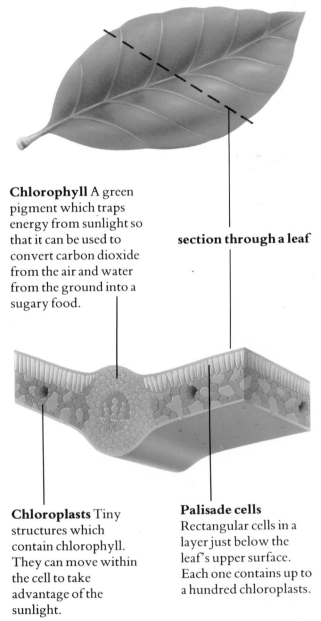

section through a leaf

Chlorophyll A green pigment which traps energy from sunlight so that it can be used to convert carbon dioxide from the air and water from the ground into a sugary food.

Chloroplasts Tiny structures which contain chlorophyll. They can move within the cell to take advantage of the sunlight.

Palisade cells Rectangular cells in a layer just below the leaf's upper surface. Each one contains up to a hundred chloroplasts.

Meat-eaters, parasites, and saprophytes

Some plants make their own food by photosynthesis, but they also eat insects for extra nourishment. These are the carnivorous plants. They often live in damp places where the ground is not very rich in minerals. Carnivorous plants have various ways of trapping their insect prey. Then they digest it over several days, dissolving its body with special digestive juices.

Other plants are what is known as parasitic or saprophytic. Saprophytes, such as most fungi, live off dead or decaying matter. This might be old leaves on the forest floor or rotting fruit. Fungi are made up of masses of tiny threads called hyphae. The hyphae run through the food and digest it.

Parasitic plants feed off living plants or animals. Mistletoe and dodder are two common parasitic plants. They climb over their host plant and take up water and food through suckers attached to the host plant.

Common butterwort The flat rosette of leaves of this carnivorous plant is covered by tiny glands which secrete a type of glue and digestive juices. Insects stick to the leaves and are trapped. The leaves curl inward to cover and digest their prey.

Fly agaric
POISONOUS. This fungus is often found under birch trees. It has a bright red cap, sometimes with white spots on it, and has white gills.

Common dodder
This parasitic plant climbs up other plants, such as nettles, shrubs and herbs. As it climbs, it sends down tiny suckers into the plant to suck up food.

Growing toward the light

Sunlight is a vital ingredient in photosynthesis and plants will always try to grow toward the light. Have a look at potted plants growing in your house. Do they lean toward the sunlight?

You could also try this experiment to see how important light is. Fit two pieces of cardboard inside a shoe box, so that each has a gap at one end. Cut a hole in one end of the box to let the light in. Then put a sprouting potato in the other end of the box. Keep the lid on the box for a few days. When you open it up, you will find that the potato has grown around the cardboard obstacles in its search for light.

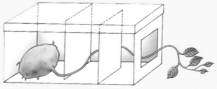

11

Why do plants have leaves?

Leaves come in a huge range of sizes and shapes but they all have one main function, to make food. Apart from this, plants breathe through their leaves (respiration) and lose water vapor through them (transpiration). In flowering plants, these leaf shapes can be divided into two basic types, which help in identifying which plant you are looking at. These are simple leaves with single leaf blades, and compound leaves with lots of small leaflets on one stalk.

Leaves provide excellent clues about the identity of a plant. Look at their size and shape, how they are arranged on the stem, and at the pattern of their veins. Many leaves have special features to help them survive in a particular habitat. See if you can spot them.

Parts of a leaf

Veins Veins carry water, minerals, and food around the leaf. They also act as skeletons, which strengthen the leaf. The vein system of a leaf is called its venation. Some leaves, for example grasses, have long, parallel veins. Most leaves have branching veins, as this leaf does.

small veins

Margin This varies in shape. It may be smooth, jagged, or lobed, or a mixture of two of these.

Midrib The central vein of the leaf is the midrib. It extends from the leaf stalk.

apex (leaf point)

Petiole The petiole brings water from the branch or stem and helps the leaf move toward the sunlight. Some leaves join the stem directly, without a petiole.

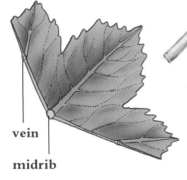

vein

midrib

Epidermis The epidermis is the outer layer of cells covering the leaf and all parts of the plant. It often has a waxy surface.

Stomata These tiny holes in the epidermis are mainly underneath the leaf. They open to allow gases in and out for photosynthesis and respiration, and water vapor out in the process of transpiration. Otherwise they remain closed to stop water loss.

Types of leaves

Pine Pines and many other conifers have narrow needles as leaves. They are mostly evergreen and are designed for survival in cold places. Because they are flexible, they bend rather than break after heavy snowfall. Pine needles are also waxy to prevent them drying out in the wind.

Holly Holly produces tough, waxy evergreen leaves to survive the cold and wind. The sharp spines around the leaf edge are to keep hungry animals off. Leaves near the bottom of the tree are spinier than those higher up, as they are most at risk.

Canadian pondweed This plant lives in streams and rivers. It has long, thin leaves to allow the plant to take in as much carbon dioxide as possible. Pondweed is a vital plant in ponds and rivers because it puts a lot of oxygen back into the water.

AMAZING FACTS

The giant Amazonian water lily has huge leaves, nearly 8 feet wide. They are big enough and strong enough for babies to sit on.

A chemical extracted from the Madagascar rosy periwinkle is used in some cures for childhood leukemia.

Koalas in Australia only eat eucalyptus leaves. The koalas sometimes smell of the strong oils contained in the leaves.

An oak tree may have over 250,000 leaves.

The largest leaves of any plants belong to the raffia palm. They can grow up to 65 feet long.

Some insects mimic leaves to camouflage themselves. The dead-leaf butterfly hides from enemies by looking exactly like a dead leaf on a branch.

The *Welwitschia mirabilis* of the Namib Desert only grows one pair of leaves in its lifetime. It takes 100 years to grow to its full size.

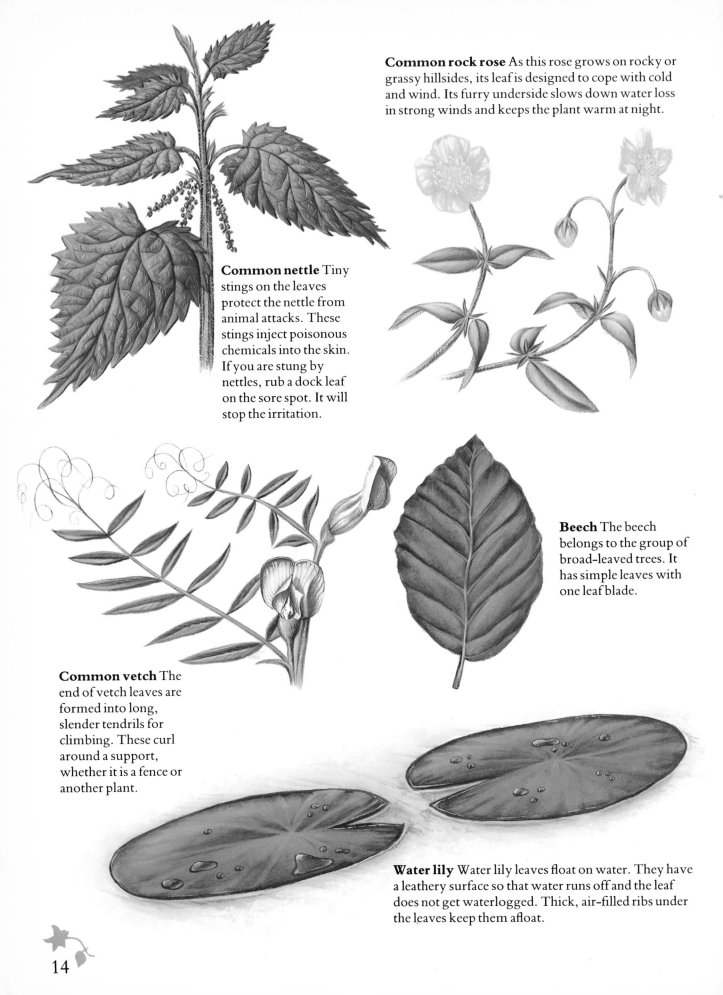

Common rock rose As this rose grows on rocky or grassy hillsides, its leaf is designed to cope with cold and wind. Its furry underside slows down water loss in strong winds and keeps the plant warm at night.

Common nettle Tiny stings on the leaves protect the nettle from animal attacks. These stings inject poisonous chemicals into the skin. If you are stung by nettles, rub a dock leaf on the sore spot. It will stop the irritation.

Beech The beech belongs to the group of broad-leaved trees. It has simple leaves with one leaf blade.

Common vetch The end of vetch leaves are formed into long, slender tendrils for climbing. These curl around a support, whether it is a fence or another plant.

Water lily Water lily leaves float on water. They have a leathery surface so that water runs off and the leaf does not get waterlogged. Thick, air-filled ribs under the leaves keep them afloat.

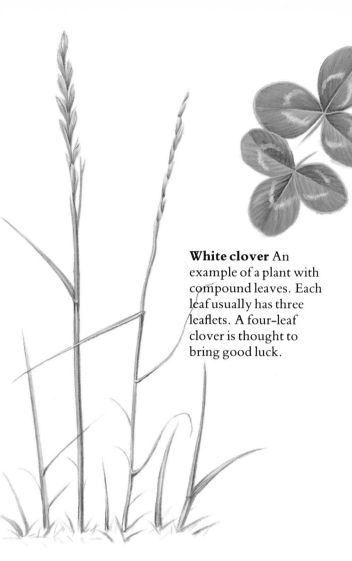

White clover An example of a plant with compound leaves. Each leaf usually has three leaflets. A four-leaf clover is thought to bring good luck.

Cacti spines

Some plants have leaves which are so highly adapted that they do not look like leaves anymore. Do you have any cacti plants at home? If not, look at a selection in your local garden center. Cacti live in dry deserts, where juicy leaves would be quickly eaten by animals for the water in them. Large leaves would also lose a lot of water across their surface. So cacti leaves have developed into prickly spines to keep animals away and reduce water loss. The spines protect the stem where many cacti store water.

Couch grass Grasses have narrow leaf blades with a parallel pattern of veins. Where the lower part of the leaf joins the stem, it forms a ridge, called a ligule. Use the shape of the ligule to identify which grass it is.

Looking at leaves

then be easier to tape into a notebook or scrapbook.

Build up a collection of leaves, from different trees and from various times of the year. To prevent the leaves curling up and drying out, press them between sheets of blotting paper. Weigh them down with a brick or heavy book and leave them for a couple of weeks. They will

You could also make leaf prints of the leaves in your collection. This is a good way of studying their vein patterns. Place the leaves on a board and cover them with a thin piece of white paper, taped down at the corners. Using a soft, thick pencil, rub over the paper so that the leaf's shape and venation show through.

What are flowers for?

A flower's main function is to produce seeds which will grow into new plants. Flowers contain a plant's reproductive parts. Some flowers contain both male and female parts. Others contain one or the other. All of them need to transfer pollen grains from the male parts to the female parts before seeds are produced. This transfer is called pollination.

Most plants cross-pollinate. This means that they need pollen from another similar plant to make seeds. They rely on the wind, water, and, most importantly, insects, to carry pollen to and fro. A flower's shape, structure, smell, and color indicate how it is pollinated. Wind-pollinated flowers may be dull and drab because they do not need to attract pollinators. But insect-pollinated flowers usually have bright petals, a sweet smell, and a store of sugary nectar to tempt bees and butterflies to them. These features are also excellent clues to a plant's identity.

The parts of a flower

Anther Pollen grains are produced by the anther.

Stamen These are the male reproductive parts of the plant. They are made up of a filament and an anther.

Petal Petals grow around the flower's reproductive parts. They are often brightly colored and scented to attract insects for pollination.

Filament The filament holds the anther up so it is easier for insects to reach the pollen.

Sepal Leaflike structures which grow around and protect the flower bud. They sometimes look very similar to petals.

Carpel This is the female reproductive part of the plant. It is made up of an ovary, a stigma and a style.

Style This joins the stigma to the ovary.

Ovary The ovary contains tiny ovules. A pollen grain must join with an ovule to make a seed.

Stigma The stigma has a sticky surface for catching pollen grains during pollination.

Receptacle The top of the flower stalk, which bears all parts of the flower.

Nectary The nectary is the area at the base of the flower where nectar, a sugary liquid, is made. Insects visit flowers to drink the nectar and become dusted with pollen from the anthers or dust pollen off on the stigmas.

16

Flowers and pollinators

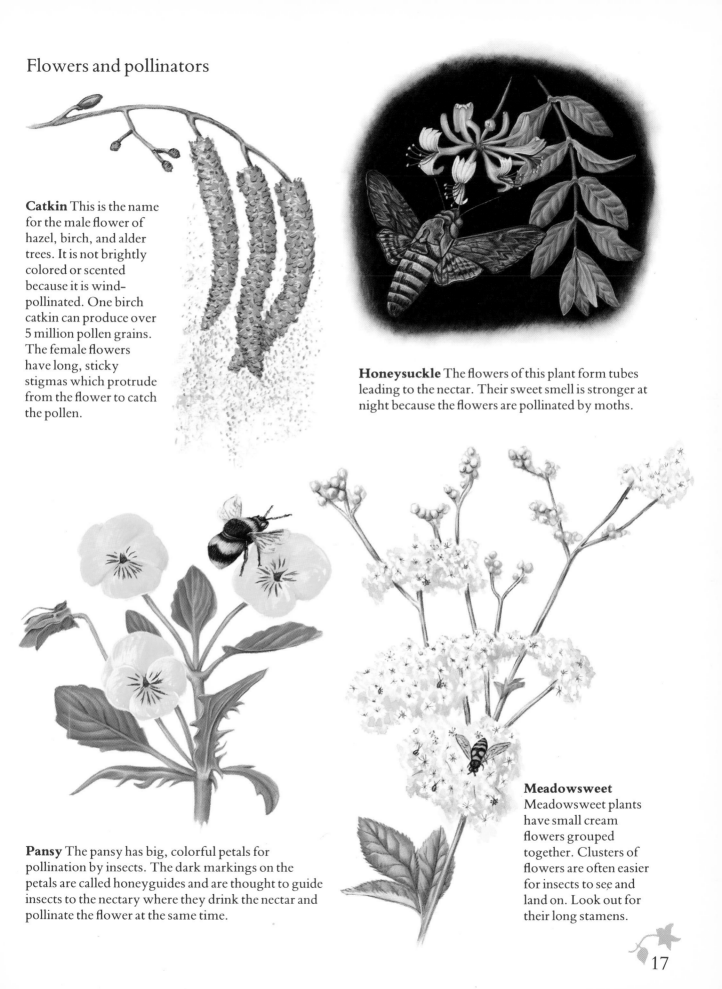

Catkin This is the name for the male flower of hazel, birch, and alder trees. It is not brightly colored or scented because it is wind-pollinated. One birch catkin can produce over 5 million pollen grains. The female flowers have long, sticky stigmas which protrude from the flower to catch the pollen.

Honeysuckle The flowers of this plant form tubes leading to the nectar. Their sweet smell is stronger at night because the flowers are pollinated by moths.

Pansy The pansy has big, colorful petals for pollination by insects. The dark markings on the petals are called honeyguides and are thought to guide insects to the nectary where they drink the nectar and pollinate the flower at the same time.

Meadowsweet Meadowsweet plants have small cream flowers grouped together. Clusters of flowers are often easier for insects to see and land on. Look out for their long stamens.

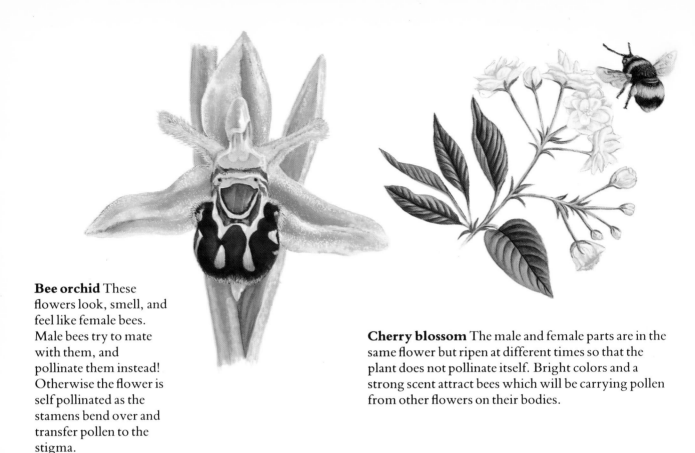

Bee orchid These flowers look, smell, and feel like female bees. Male bees try to mate with them, and pollinate them instead! Otherwise the flower is self pollinated as the stamens bend over and transfer pollen to the stigma.

Cherry blossom The male and female parts are in the same flower but ripen at different times so that the plant does not pollinate itself. Bright colors and a strong scent attract bees which will be carrying pollen from other flowers on their bodies.

Wildflower watch

A good way of studying wildflowers is to let a small patch of your garden grow wild. Clear a patch of garden in early summer and watch how quickly plants start growing in it. You could also sow some wildflower seeds to give more variety. Record the progress of these plants using a quadrat, or square frame, made of four 3-feet long pieces of wood. Divide the quadrat into 16 squares with pieces of string and put it over your garden patch. Draw a corresponding grid on a piece of paper. Note down the plants growing in each different square. You could do this once a month for a really detailed wildflower survey. Keep a close watch, too, on the types of insects that visit the flowers.

Grass flowers

Grasses are the most common flowering plants in the world and the type you are most likely to see on a walk in the town or country. There are over 10,000 species of grass, ranging from wheat and rye, to bamboo and sugarcane, to the grass on your lawn at home.

Grasses flower from about May to July. The flowers are pollinated by the wind and have no petals. The flowers are grouped in spikelets. These will help you to identify the various types of grass.

Rye grass To identify this type of grass, look out for flat, oval spikelets arranged alternately on the spike with up to ten flowers.

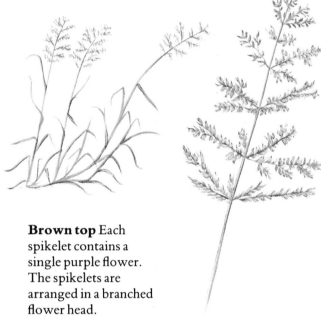

Brown top Each spikelet contains a single purple flower. The spikelets are arranged in a branched flower head.

Squirrel tail This grass has pairs of bristly spikelets on a stiff spike.

AMAZING FACTS

The rafflesia plant produces the heaviest, and smelliest, flowers. Each can measure up to 3 feet across and weigh almost 15 pounds. The flowers' rotting-meat smell attracts flies for pollination. The flies land in the hope of finding food.

The lords and ladies flower attracts midges by giving off a strong scent. The midges slide down the slippery sides of the leaflike structure surrounding the flower and are trapped inside. They are released the next day which ensures that they will have unloaded any pollen they were carrying.

The smallest flowering plant is an aquatic duckweed from Australia. It is smaller than the period at the end of this sentence.

Fruits and seeds

Seeds and dispersal

Once pollination has happened and the pollen has fertilized the ovule, a seed grows. It contains a new plant and a store of food to give the plant enough energy to grow until the shoots and leaves start making food themselves. The ovary develops into a protective fruit around the seeds. The fruit may be a berry, a pod, or a nut.

The size, shape, texture, and color of a plant's fruit are good clues about how its seeds are scattered. Plants cannot move so, as with pollination, they have to get the wind, water, birds, and insects to disperse their seeds for them. Many fruits have special features according to which dispersal method is used. Fleshy fruits such as cherries, for instance, are sweet tasting to encourage birds to eat them. Hopefully the bird will carry the cherry away and discard the seed inside it on fertile ground away from the parent plant.

Parts of a seed

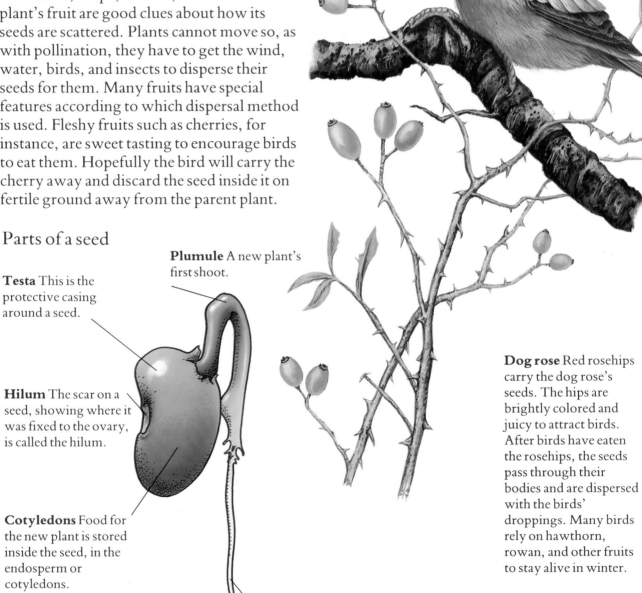

Plumule A new plant's first shoot.

Testa This is the protective casing around a seed.

Hilum The scar on a seed, showing where it was fixed to the ovary, is called the hilum.

Cotyledons Food for the new plant is stored inside the seed, in the endosperm or cotyledons.

Radicle A new plant's first root.

Dog rose Red rosehips carry the dog rose's seeds. The hips are brightly colored and juicy to attract birds. After birds have eaten the rosehips, the seeds pass through their bodies and are dispersed with the birds' droppings. Many birds rely on hawthorn, rowan, and other fruits to stay alive in winter.

Hazel The seeds are contained inside thick, tough shells. Mammals, such as squirrels, carry off the fallen nuts. Some they eat, but others are stored for later in the year. If they are forgotten about, some of these seeds will survive to grow into new plants.

California poppy The seeds are contained in the seed head. As the wind shakes the seed head, the seeds are sprinkled on the ground. You can tell when a poppy is ready to disperse its seeds because the seeds rattle around inside the seed head.

AMAZING FACTS

The biggest seed is that of the coco-de-mer palm which only grows on the Seychelle Islands. A single seed can weigh up to 40 pounds and may take 20 years to ripen.

Orchids produce the smallest seeds. Some orchid seeds are so tiny that 1.25 million seeds would weigh just 1 gram.

In 1966, scientists germinated some Arctic lupine seeds they had found frozen in the ground in Canada. The seeds thought to be as much as 15,000 years old, yet some still sprouted and grew.

As its name suggests, the squirting cucumber squirts its seeds out. They shoot out at such a speed that if you are standing in the way, they would hurt you!

Sycamore The fruits, or keys, have wings so that they can be easily carried away by the wind. The keys of the maple tree are also scattered by the wind.

Dandelion Dandelions rely on the wind to spread their seeds. The seeds are attached to tiny, fluffy parachutes which are carried away by the slightest breeze.

Tufted vetch The seeds are contained in pods. As these pods dry out in the sun, they suddenly snap open and shoot the seeds out to disperse them. Broom pods behave in a similar way.

Growing plants from seeds

The best way to see how a new plant grows from a seed is to try growing a pea or runner bean seed. Line a glass jar with damp blotting paper and place the pea or bean between the paper and the glass. Leave it in the dark until it sprouts. Keep the blotting paper damp.

The skin around the bean (the testa) will split open and the radicle should grow, followed by the plumule. The bean uses up its food store until its leaves open and it can photosynthesize. The process of a seed growing into a new plant is called germination.

When your bean has sprouted, plant it in a pot or in the garden. If the weather and soil are right, it will flower in about six weeks. Don't forget that peas and beans are climbing plants, so you will need to build them a stick support to grow up.

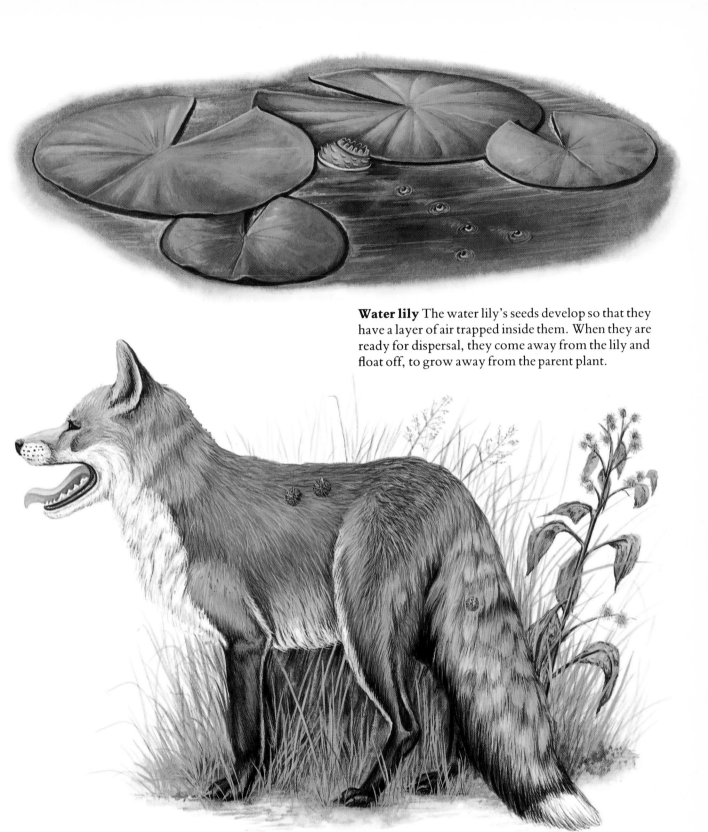

Water lily The water lily's seeds develop so that they have a layer of air trapped inside them. When they are ready for dispersal, they come away from the lily and float off, to grow away from the parent plant.

Common burdock The burdock's fruit are called burrs. They are covered in tiny hooks which catch on the wool or fur of passing animals. Eventually the burrs fall off or are scratched off by the animals, and seeds scatter on the ground.

Going underground

So far, your detective work has been concentrated on the parts of the plant that show above ground. However, there is a great deal going on underground, too. Roots anchor the plant firmly in the ground and take in the water and minerals it needs to make food. In some plants, the roots also swell during the summer to store enough food to see the plant through to the next year. Many of the vegetables we eat, such as carrots and radishes, are, in fact, roots.

Although you should never uproot wild plants, you can take a closer look at roots when you are weeding in the garden. Also, after a heavy storm, you may see trees uprooted by the wind. You can then examine their spreading root system.

Parts of a root

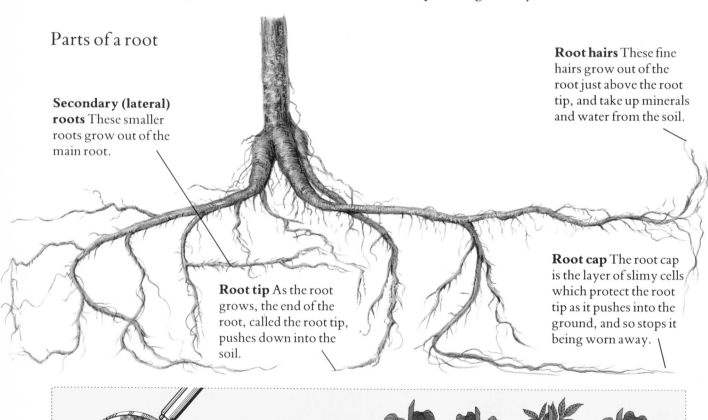

Secondary (lateral) roots These smaller roots grow out of the main root.

Root hairs These fine hairs grow out of the root just above the root tip, and take up minerals and water from the soil.

Root tip As the root grows, the end of the root, called the root tip, pushes down into the soil.

Root cap The root cap is the layer of slimy cells which protect the root tip as it pushes into the ground, and so stops it being worn away.

Making a plant take root

To see how plants grow roots, take some cuttings from a house plant, such as a geranium, impatiens, or spiderwort. Cut a 4-inch length from the plant's stem.

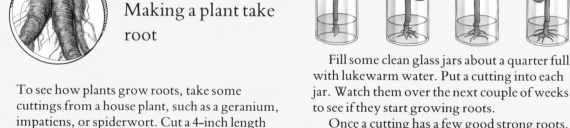

Fill some clean glass jars about a quarter full with lukewarm water. Put a cutting into each jar. Watch them over the next couple of weeks to see if they start growing roots.

Once a cutting has a few good strong roots, take it out of the water and plant it carefully in a pot of soil, mixed with some potting compost.

Plants underground

Potato The potato's tuber is a short, swollen underground stem. Here the plant stores starchy food to nourish new shoots sprouting from the tuber.

Tropical orchids In tropical climates, some plants have developed aerial roots. These grow from the plant's stem into the air, and take in water vapor present in the humid air.

Clover Small swellings, called nodules, on the roots of clover and other legumes, contain bacteria which convert nitrogen in the air into a nutrient for the plant. Some of this nutrient is released into the surrounding soil and so acts as a fertilizer for other plants. For this reason, clover is often planted alongside other plants in order to provide them with nitrogen nourishment. Look out for root nodules on pea and bean plants and on lupines, too.

Garlic These bulbs are swollen leaves around a short stem. The leaves store the sugary food that the plant uses to grow. The following year, a new plant grows out of the bulb. Onions, daffodils, and tulips are some of the many plants that produce bulbs.

Fern The rhizome is a thick stem which grows horizontally under the ground. It produces roots and shoots which grow into new plants. Irises and grasses also produce rhizomes.

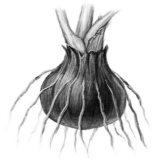

Crocus The corm is a short stem, like a bulb, but the food is stored in the stem itself, not in the leaves around it. Again, a new plant develops from the corm the next year.

AMAZING FACTS

A wild fig tree growing in Echo Caves, South Africa, has the deepest roots of any plant known. They are 400 feet long.

Some mangroves have special roots to help them survive in salty estuaries. Too much salt can kill plants. The mangroves have roots which filter salt out of the water as they suck it up. They also have some special roots, which grow above the water surface to take up air.

Scientists studying a young rye plant found that it produced 3 miles of roots a day for every day of its life.

Plants without flowers

Some plants do not have flowers so they reproduce in different ways. Conifers produce their seeds in cones while ferns, mosses, horsetails, and club mosses reproduce with tiny, specklike spores instead of seeds. These are released in the thousands and carried away by the wind to grow into new plants, if they land in a suitable place.

Fungi are different from flowering and nonflowering plants. As they do not contain chlorophyll, they cannot make their own food. Instead, they live on the debris of other living plants and animals (see page 11).

Marchantia polymorpha This liverwort lives along the banks of rivers and streams, in damp places in the garden and in greenhouses. Its spore capsules grow underneath female "umbrellas."

Mosses and liverworts

These are small, ground-hugging plants which live in damp places. They have to keep damp as they do not have a waxy covering which would stop them from drying out. They do not have proper roots either. The spores form in a spore capsule, held up on a stalk. The shape of the capsule is a good way of identifying the various species.

Bryum capillare This grows in clumps on walls, roofs, rocks, and sometimes tree stumps. It can be recognized by its pear-shaped spore capsule which changes from green to brown.

Lichen

Lichens are made up of two plants – a fungus and an alga – living in partnership. The alga provides the fungus with food made by photosynthesis, and the fungus provides protection and water for the alga.

Xanthoria parietina This is a crusty yellow lichen which often grows on old walls and rocks. It can turn rocks to soil over a long period of time, by sending out acids which eat into the rock and make it crumble. The lichen then takes in minerals from the rocks for nourishment.

AMAZING FACTS

Ringworm and athlete's foot are caused by fungi, which live off people's skin.

Fungi produce huge numbers of spores. Giant puffballs measure about 6 feet across. They can produce an amazing 7 trillion spores. Even an ordinary field mushroom produces about 3 million spores a week.

In the prehistoric forests, giant horsetails grew 150 feet tall, higher than a 10-story building.

Algae

Algae are very simple, flowerless plants. They do not have roots and their bodies are not divided into leaves and stems. They range from microscopic, one-celled plants to huge seaweeds. They are classed according to their color – green, red, or brown. All algae contain chlorophyll. The other pigments help them to absorb more sunlight to make food. They usually live in water.

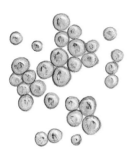

Chlamydomonas This single-celled green alga lives in fresh water. It is microscopic but it reproduces in such large numbers in summer that it colors the water green. An "orange spot" inside the cell senses the direction of the sunlight.

Bladder wrack
Bladder wrack is a member of the brown algae, the group which includes the largest seaweeds. It is found on seashores and rocks. Fronds have air-filled pouches which help them to float. The fronds are very tough to survive being battered by the tide.

Irish moss A common red alga of rock pools and rocky seashores. The fronds of this edible seaweed can reach 6 inches long. Seaweeds attach themselves to rocks with round structures, called holdfasts.

Fungi

Fungi have no flowers or leaves and no proper roots or stems. Some fungi produce fruiting bodies which appear above ground as toadstools or mushrooms. Spores grow under the cap of the mushroom or toadstool, on ridges called gills. The color of the spores and the shape and pattern of the gills are good ways of identifying the different types of fungi. If you are interested in mushrooms and fungi, borrow a field guide from the library so that you can identify them.

WARNING! WARNING! Although some fungi are edible, many are highly poisonous. To be on the safe side, never pick fungi to eat.

Velvet shank You may find this fungus growing on the trunks of dead trees. It is distinguished by its yellowy orange cap, dark brown stem, and pale yellow gills.

Puffball The main body of a puffball looks like a round, smooth ball. It is found on the ground in fields and woods. Puffballs release their spores in puffs into the air. The wind carries them away.

Death cap HIGHLY POISONOUS. The death cap lives in deciduous woodland. It can be recognized by its greenish yellow cap and white gills.

Ferns, horsetails, and club mosses

Ferns are easily identified by their leafy fronds, rising from underground stems. Some ferns have their spore-bearing structures, called sori, on the underside of all their leaves. Sori often look like a patch of rust. You can use the shape and arrangement of the sori to help you identify the different types of fern. Other ferns have special leaves or separate stems for the spore-bearing structures.

Horsetails and club mosses belong to a very ancient group of plants. Their ancestors grew up to 100 feet tall, some 300 million years ago. They formed huge, swampy forests. When they died, their remains turned into coal. Horsetails and club mosses produce their spores in conelike structures, as ferns do.

Bracken Bracken is very common in woods and dry meadows. It reproduces by spores and by rhizome (see page 25). It has triangular leaf fronds. The sori grow in a line along the edges of the pinnules.

Staghorn club moss This is found in woods and along rocky slopes. The spores are contained in slim, yellowish cones on the branches.

Swamp horsetail As its name suggests, this horsetail lives at the water's edge. Cones grow at the tips of the stems and can be almost an inch long.

Male fern This fern is very common in woods and hedgerows. The leaf fronds are divided into lobes (pinnae) with smaller lobes (pinnules). Sori are arranged in two rows of between six and eight, under each pinnule.

Conifers

Conifers have cones instead of flowers or fruit. A pinecone takes about three years to grow. At first, it is small, green, and soft. Then it hardens and turns brown. Inside the scales, the seeds are protected. Finally when the weather is dry and the seeds stand a chance of surviving, the cones open up to release the seeds. In wet weather, they stay closed to keep the seeds warm and dry. You can test this for yourself by putting a pinecone near a warm radiator. It should open its scales. If you put it in a damp place it will close them again.

Norway spruce This tree can be identified by its stiff, dark green needles and its long, hanging cones. These are slightly flexible. The Norway spruce is the traditional Christmas tree that we bring inside and decorate.

Douglas fir The needles of this conifer are soft and give off a pleasant fragrance. The adult cones (above) are a brownish color and can be identified by their slightly shaggy appearance. This is due to tufts, called bracts, hanging off them.

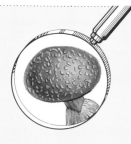

Making spore prints

You can look at gill patterns by making spore prints. To make a spore print, find a firm, ripe mushroom and cut the stem off with a knife. Place the cap gill-side down on a piece of paper.

Use black paper for mushrooms with white gills and white paper for mushrooms with dark gills.

Leave the cap for a few hours, or overnight if you can. Then, carefully lift up the cap and you should have a spore print on the paper. To stop your print smudging, spray it with a fixative spray. You can buy this from an art shop. Always use it in a well-ventilated place, away from flames. Never breathe the spray in.

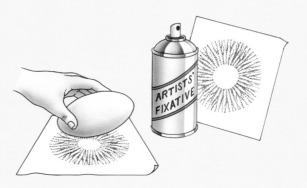

More things to do

Making bark rubbings

You can recognize different types of tree by their bark. Look at the bark's color and texture. Is it smooth or cracked and grooved? Does it have any other special patterns? Is it peeling off the tree in strips or breaking off in flakes? You should never peel bark off a tree because this can kill it. But you can take a bark rubbing instead. Tape a piece of waxed paper to the tree trunk. Rub over it firmly with a soft wax crayon. Be careful not to tear the paper. Don't forget to write the type of tree on each rubbing, if you know it.

Collecting dried flowers

You should never pick rare wildflowers, but make a collection of some more common ones, from your garden. The weeds in your garden are the wildflowers in the countryside. Then, press them so that you can study them later. You can buy special flower presses or you could make your own. Put your flowers between two sheets of blotting paper, then between two sheets of light wood. Tape the wood together, and put the whole press under a pile of heavy books or weights. Leave the press for two to three weeks to make sure the flower is completely dried. Remove it gently and tape into a scrapbook or folder. Remember to make a note of where you found it, when you found it, and what it is called.

Lichen alert

Even if you live in a crowded city, you should be able to find some lichens growing on stone or brick walls, tree trunks, and even tombstones. These plants are very sensitive to pollution and you can use them to test how clean the air is. Use this scale to help you.

Lichen

State of the air

Clean

Green, leafy lichen
Shrubby lichen

Slightly dirtier

Crusty, orange or grayish green lichen

No lichens

Very dirty

Garden in a bottle

To make a bottle garden you will need:
a large glass jar or bottle, with an airtight lid
small pebbles
potting compost

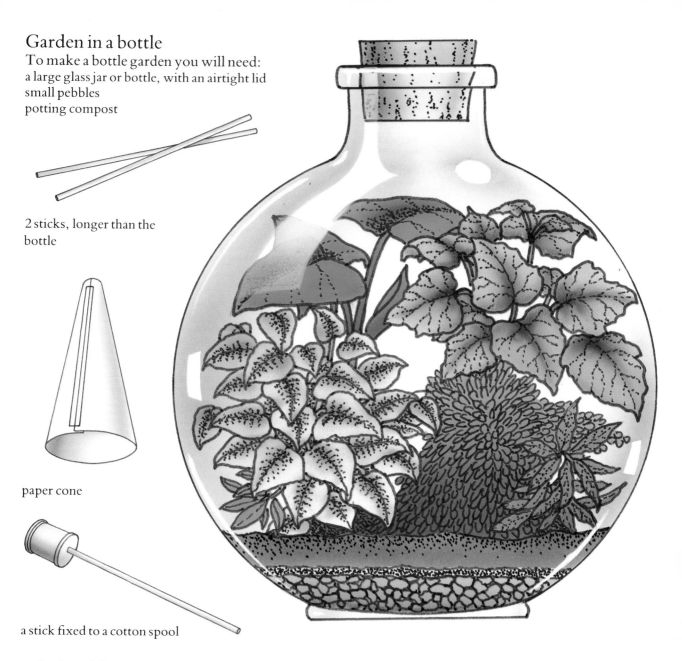

2 sticks, longer than the bottle

paper cone

a stick fixed to a cotton spool

a selection of plants, such as small ferns, African violet, ivy, mosses, small palms.

What to do:
1. Carefully drop enough pebbles into the bottle to cover the bottom.
2. Using the paper cone as a funnel, pour the potting compost into the bottle. It should be 1 or 2 inches deep, depending on how big the bottle is.
3. For each plant, make a hole in the compost with a stick, then use both sticks to lower the plant into the bottle. Firm the soil down with the cotton spool.
4. Spray the plants with water, and leave them to grow, remembering to water them regularly.

Measuring trees

To measure the height of a tree, you will need a tape measure and a friend! Ask your friend to stand next to the tree, holding one end of the tape measure at the base of the trunk. You should take the other end of the measure and start walking away from the tree. After every couple of steps, bend down and look back between your legs. When you can just see the top of the tree between your legs, stop and look at the tape measure. How far have you walked? The distance back to the tree is about the same as the height of the tree.

Index